THE LEAF DETECTIVE

HOW MARGARET LOWMAN UNCOVERED SECRETS IN THE RAINFOREST

Heather Lang

Illustrated by Jana Christy

CALKINS CREEK
AN IMPRINT OF ASTRA BOOKS FOR YOUNG READERS
New York

To my sister Melinda—
for all you do to make our world a better place
        —HL

For Harry and Hugo, who helped me love trees even more
        —JC

The author is donating a portion of her royalties to Meg Lowman's TREE Foundation.

For information about permission to reproduce selections from this book,
please contact permissions@astrapublishinghouse.com.

Calkins Creek
An imprint of Astra Books for Young Readers, a division of Astra Publishing House
astrapublishinghouse.com
Printed in China

ISBN: 978-1-68437-177-8 (hc) / 978-1-63592-369-8 (eBook)
Library of Congress Control Number: 2019956448

First edition
10 9 8 7 6 5 4 3

Design by Barbara Grzeslo
The type is set in Avenir.
The illustrations are created digitally.

"WE ARE *PART* OF OUR ECOSYSTEM, NOT OUTSIDE IT."

—Margaret "Canopy Meg" Lowman

Meg loved how leaves
burst into the world
and unfurled.
She admired their different shapes,
colors, and textures.

After twenty years of thinking about them,
  reading about them,
    studying them,
Meg wanted to *understand* them,
to discover their stories.
How did they survive?
  How long did they live?
  Why did they die?

But looking at leaves from the ground
gets a rainforest scientist only so far.
Meg knew she had to find a way
to go *to* the leaves—
to the treetops.

"WE HAD ALREADY BEEN TO THE MOON AND BACK AND NOBODY
HAD BEEN TO THE TOP OF A TREE."

Before 1979, most scientists studied
rainforest treetops through binoculars. Some
also cut trees down or sprayed them with
chemicals and collected the dead leaves
(and insects) that fell to the ground.

Meg Lowman had been a leaf detective
ever since she was a young girl,
in the 1950s
in Elmira, New York.

Shy and studious,
Meg rarely spoke in school.

"IT PAINED ME IF I WAS EVER CALLED UPON IN CLASS."

Instead,
she found comfort and friendship
and quiet excitement
in plants.

She built tree forts and
collected twigs, leaves,
and wildflowers
to study and identify,
to press and label:
    swamp thistle,
      devil's paintbrush,
        forget-me-nots.

"I WAS LITERALLY THE ONLY ONE IN MY
TOWN LIKE MYSELF."

Meg wrapped herself in nature,
like a soft blanket.

YARROW

In college Meg fed her passion with science—
she was a young woman in a jungle of men
with no women to lead the way.

One professor refused to let her in his class,
because she was a woman.

$$p_1 + \varrho g y_1 + \tfrac{1}{2}\varrho v_1^2 = p_2 + \varrho g y_2 + \tfrac{1}{2}\varrho v_2^2$$

$$V = \frac{\pi}{2}$$

$$Y = \frac{F}{J}$$

$$\frac{F}{A} = E \frac{\Delta l}{l_0}$$

$$\sigma = E \varepsilon$$

Still she stuck like sap to her passion
and followed it to graduate school
and the tropical rainforests of Australia.

No one at Sydney University
had studied the rainforest before.

Tropical rainforests receive at least
sixty inches of rain per year. The hot, humid
environment encourages lots of different
plants to grow. This diversity supports a
huge variety of animal species.

In the dark, damp forest
the trees rose up to
distant rustling,
squawks and screeches,
shadows in the treetops.

How could she get up there?

Using seat-belt straps,
Meg sewed a harness.
From a metal rod,
she welded a slingshot.

Pull, aim, release, fire . . .
Meg launched a lead weight on a line
again and again
until at last it caught
around the sturdy branch of a coachwood tree.

Most rainforest trees are between sixty and one hundred and fifty feet tall. Their branches form the canopy—a big umbrella that shades the forest floor.

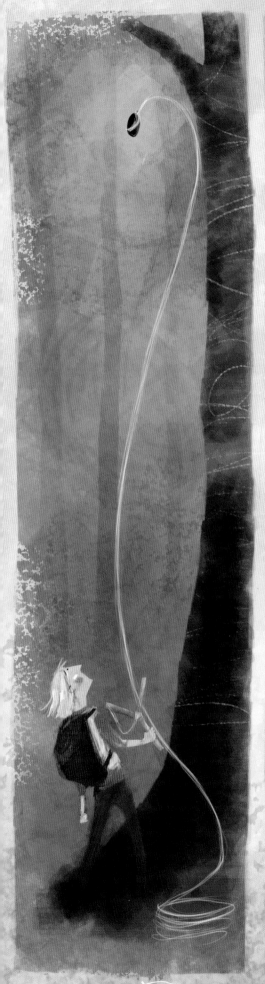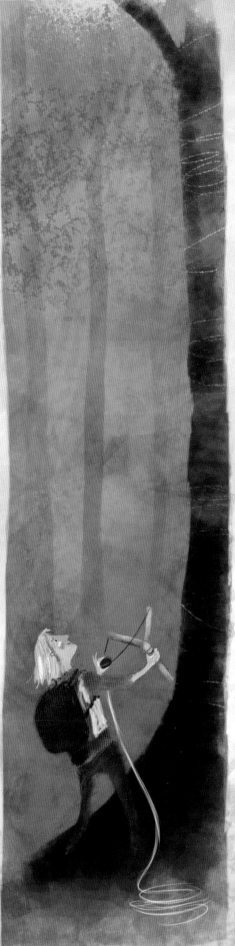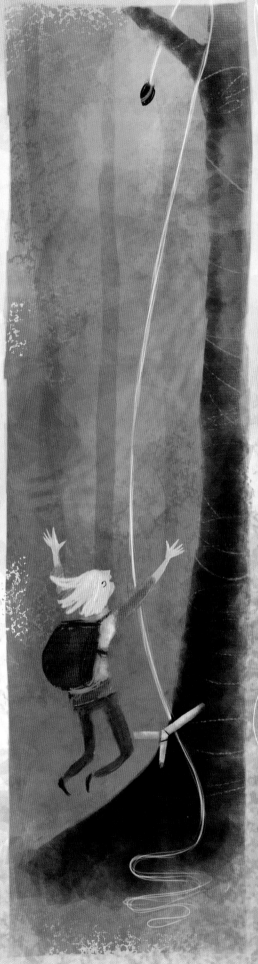

At first Meg flailed.
Upside down, right-side up.
The steamy forest painted her
with a coat of sweat.
Swinging and twisting, she dangled
like a worm on a hook.

"I WAS FROZEN WITH FEAR."

Meg inched up the rope.
But she worried:
What if the branch breaks?
  Will my sewing hold up?
    Will a bird peck through my rope?

What sits waiting in the treetops?

At last, splashed with flowers and sunlight—
 the canopy!
The treetop swayed
 back and forth.
Flies whizzed. Lizards lingered.
A black weevil sucked leaf juices.
Sweat bees landed on her arm
for a lick of salt.
And the jungle's music danced all around her.

"FROM THEN ON, I NEVER LOOKED BACK . . . OR DOWN!"

Insects eat leaves by chewing them, piercing and sucking from the leaf, or tunneling in and eating the inside of the leaf.

To Meg it was a secret world,
with brilliant parrots and sleepy koalas,
slithering pythons and busy ants.

And leaves—
lovely leaves!
Large and small,
shiny and prickly,
tender and tough.

To scientists it was a new frontier—
mysterious
and unexplored.

We now believe the canopy is home to approximately half the plant and animal species on land.

Many people in Australia didn't understand Meg.
They thought the rainforests were
dark and gloomy
and full of snakes.
They wanted to cut them all down.

By the 1970s, deforestation, the clearing of forests by humans, had become a serious problem in Australia and around the world. Scientists guess that more than half of our forests have already been destroyed.

"You can't do this," people said.
"You're a woman."
"Women don't climb trees."

Meg ignored them.
Rainforest mysteries
called her
to climb and discover.

She climbed the red cedar,
the Antarctic beech,
the sassafras.

She explored the stinging tree.
It defended itself—
its pincushion leaves tore at her skin,
and chemical hairs injected poisons
with a fiery sting!

"[TREES] CAN'T RUN AWAY FROM
THEIR ENEMIES LIKE ANIMALS CAN, SO
INSTEAD THEY HAVE TO MAKE A LOT
OF DEFENSES . . . THORNS . . . FUZZY
LEAVES . . . TOXINS."

Plant chemicals can be used as
medicines for humans. For example, chemicals
from the rosy periwinkle, found in Madagascar,
provide a cure for leukemia. We have learned
how to use only a very small number
of the world's medicinal plants.

On each tree
Meg numbered leaves,
on different branches
at different heights.
She monitored and traced them
to find out how long they lived.

Hour after hour, day after day, she worked
alone
in the treetops.

"I FOUND THESE TIMES ALONE TO BE VERY STRENGTHENING,
AS THEY ENCOURAGED ME TO DEVELOP CONFIDENCE IN MYSELF."

With each new climb
Meg discovered nibbled edges,
lacy skeletons,
and leaves that vanished—quick as a snake's prey.
She wondered, *What is eating all these leaves?*

One night, outside her tent,
Meg heard sounds.
In the darkness,
she crept into the forest.
Noises swarmed around her—
    munching . . .
        crunching. . .
            chewing . . .
With her headlamp,
Meg scanned the leaves of a coachwood tree
and discovered
walkingsticks and beetles feasting!

"TO MY AMAZEMENT AND DELIGHT . . .
MOST HERBIVORES FED AT NIGHT."

Herbivores are animals that eat plant material. Meg discovered that 15 to 25 percent of tropical rainforest leaves are eaten every year, mostly by insects.

To insects, a tree is *not* just a tree,
it is a "salad bar"—
all-you-can-eat leaves.

To birds and mammals, a tree is a buffet—
juicy fruits and plump beetles,
salamanders, and frogs.

A tree is a sponge,
soaking up water from the forest floor,
and a recycler,
giving water back to the clouds,
ready to quench another day's thirst.

When animals eat leaves and feed on dead
and weak trees, they return nutrients to the
soil through their digestion, nourishing trees and
future seedlings.

Trees release water from their leaves in a process called transpiration. This water forms rain clouds. Moisture from the Amazon affects rainfall as far away as Texas.

Meg tried to climb at night,
but dangling from a rope, studying leaves,
is difficult
and dangerous
in a dark forest
    with deadly snakes
        and spiders
           and ravenous biting ants.

She had to find a better way.
She brainstormed with other scientists.
She thought and imagined . . .
What if I fly up in a balloon?
Or work from the edges of hillsides?
Or train a monkey?

Then one night,
at one of her research sites,
she and a friend
had a brilliant idea—
a trail through the treetops
made with ladders instead of ropes.
They sketched the plan on a napkin.

Meg helped invent the world's first canopy walkway!

Now she could research day and night,
    in good weather and stormy,
        alone and with others.

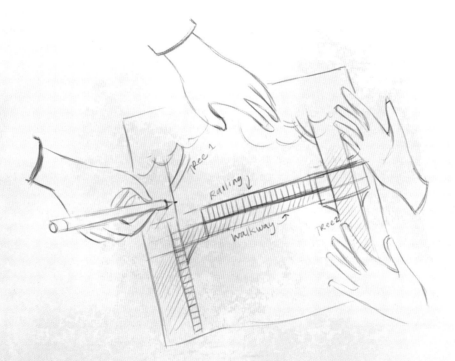

In 1988, Meg and Peter O'Reilly
designed the canopy walkway at his
Rainforest Retreat in Queensland, Australia.
It had three suspension bridges and
reached a height of one hundred
and ten feet.

Meg loved to give tours
on the canopy walkway.
Now Australian people
wanted to visit their rainforest.

Meg returned to the United States
and designed more walkways.
She experimented with other ways
to explore forest canopies.

In Cameroon, Africa,
she joined a team of scientists
who launched a hot-air balloon
that placed a raft on the treetops.
Meg couldn't wait to stand
on top of the canopy!
She had never been there before.

In the sweltering heat,
Meg struggled up the rope
through the forest's understory.
She wondered,
    What sits waiting on the treetops?
The heat drained her energy,
and she drained her water bottles.

"THE CLIMB SEEMED NEVER ENDING."

At last, Meg reached the treetops
and climbed up through a hole
onto the raft.

Spread out before her as far as she could see:
trees, trees, beautiful trees,
millions of years in the making,
filled with life,
giving life.

It can take sixty million to one hundred million years for a rainforest to form. Many of our rainforests existed when dinosaurs roamed the earth.

But it struck her:
What good is my research
for the trees,
    for the animals,
      for people,
when the chainsaws are coming?

"IF WE DO NOT CONSERVE RAIN FORESTS, ALL OF OUR DATA WILL
REFERENCE EXTINCT ORGANISMS OR SITES THAT USED TO BE."

Every minute about
thirty-four acres of forest are
destroyed—the size of twenty-six
American football fields.

To some people,
a tree is just a tree,
good for timber
or rubber
or paper.

To others, it is just a tree,
taking up land they could use
to raise cattle
and grow coffee or soybeans.

Rainforest trees clean our air, absorbing a gas called carbon dioxide and providing oxygen—the gas we breathe. When we cut down trees, they release those gases back into the atmosphere and will never again clean our air.

Back in the United States,
as she wrote up her research,
Meg worried about the trees.

She wondered,
    How can one leaf detective make a difference?
      How can I save the trees?
        I must save the trees!

Then an idea crawled into Meg's thoughts—
a way to speak for the trees.

"PLANTS GAVE ME A VOICE!"

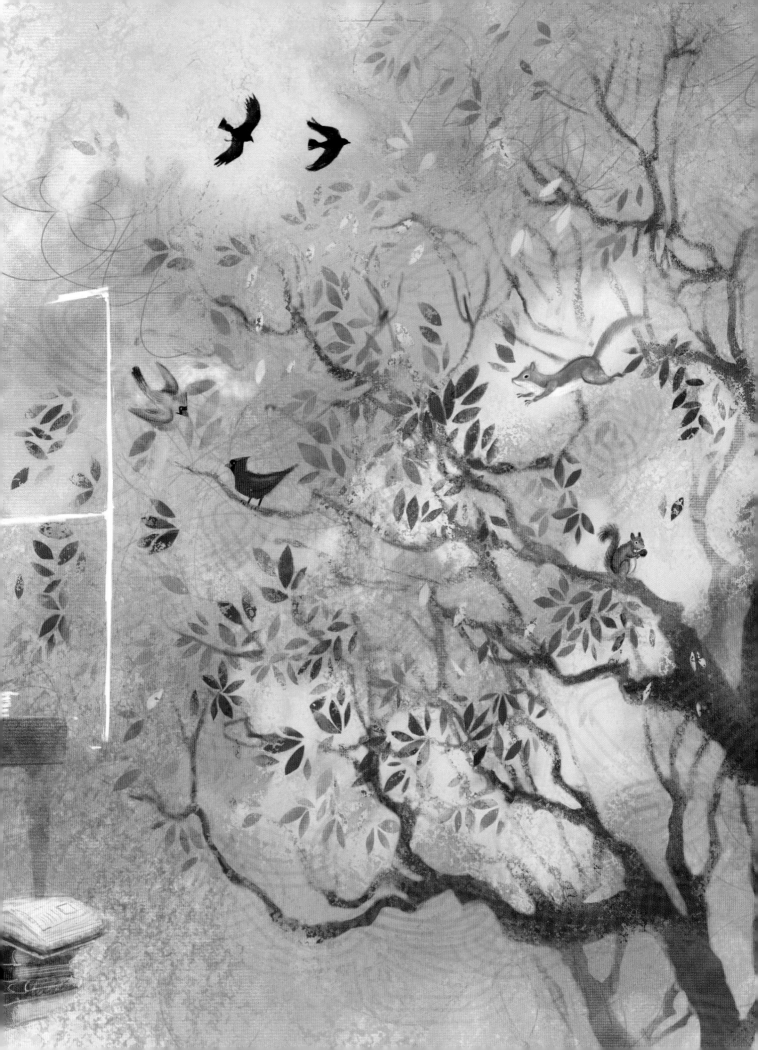

Meg traveled back to Cameroon
and spoke to the villagers
about the gifts their rainforest had to offer.
She taught them to climb trees
and survey the forests,
to identify and collect
orchids and ferns.

Now they could sell crops and plants instead of trees.

Some of our favorite treats are grown in the rainforest, including chocolate, cinnamon, and pineapples.

Meg took her battle
to other countries.

In Western Samoa
she convinced the people
to build a canopy walkway.
Now they could make money
to build a school
by sharing their rainforest
with the world
through canopy tourism.

In northern Ethiopia, most of the forests have been cleared for agriculture. The only forests left are in churchyards and cover just 5 percent of the land. Meg is working with the priests and villagers to protect these forests.

In Ethiopia
Meg persuaded the people
to gather rocks from their fields
and build stone walls
to protect their last lonely patches of trees.

"NOW, FIRST AND FOREMOST, I ASK 'HOW CAN WE SAVE IT?'
SO THAT LATER I CAN RETURN AND ASK 'WHAT AND WHY?'"

Meg used her voice
to inspire people
to save their rainforests
to save themselves,
    because to Meg, a tree is *not* just a tree.

It is a shelter for animals and people,
a recycler and provider of water,
a creator of food and oxygen,
an inventor of medicine,
a soldier against climate change.

It is essential for life on earth.

"IF ONLY I COULD HAVE ACHIEVED AS MUCH AS THE TREE! . . . BUT I HAVE NOT.
I HAVE WHITTLED AWAY AT RELATIVELY SMALL GOALS IN COMPARISON TO
THE GRANDER ACCOMPLISHMENTS OF A TREE."

AUTHOR'S NOTE

When I learned about how twenty-five-year-old Meg Lowman invented a slingshot and harness and became one of the first scientists to explore the canopy, I was in awe of her resourcefulness and raw courage. And she did it back in 1979 without ever having a single female professor or mentor. That alone could have been a book. Meg has accomplished so much, I agonized over what to include.

Meg has discovered new species, identified different plant and insect interactions, measured herbivory in forests around the world, and made countless scientific discoveries. Her canopy studies in Australia showed that leaves live as little as three months and as long as nineteen years! When I finally met Meg for an in-person interview, I realized my best way into her story was her deep love for plants and how it shaped her. Like a leaf she unfurled, gradually transforming from a shy and quiet child, who didn't know women could be scientists, into a world-class scientist, educator, and conservationist.

Meg's persistence to become a field biologist in a culture that didn't believe in female scientists was remarkable. Once her two sons were born, she had to find a way to bring them with her into the field. When James and Eddie were ages three and four, she decided to get them harnesses rather than leave them at the bottoms of the trees with the dangerous snakes! Seeing nature through their eyes helped her realize the importance of educating young people about their rainforests.

In the 1990s, Meg began working with the Jason Project, educating millions of middle-school students with virtual expeditions into the canopy. Her struggles also inspired her passion to mentor women and minorities in field biology in the United States and as far away as Ethiopia and India. And to ensure that science really is for everyone, she created a tree-climbing research program for students in wheelchairs.

In 2017, I had the thrill of learning from Meg on a citizen-scientist trip to the Amazon rainforest in Peru. Our group traced and counted leaves to help Meg measure and calculate herbivory. We met some indigenous people and learned how they live off the rainforest in sustainable ways. We soaked up her talks about leaves, plant adaptations, mutualism, and the dangers of deforestation. Meg marveled at the strength of her favorite tree—the strangler fig, which unlike other trees, starts at the top of the rainforest and drops its roots down. This tree reminds her that "taking the road less traveled has its advantages." Meg's powerful bond with plants was ever present.

My first climb into the canopy was exhilarating, and looking down from the safety of a walkway, I imagined what it must have been like for her to be up there dangling from a rope. The views and bird-watching from the canopy walkway at sunrise and sunset took my breath away. And night walks, with tarantulas, scorpions, and the loud sounds of busy animals, both excited and unnerved me.

Experiencing the rainforest with Meg as my guide is an adventure I will never forget. She has given me a new appreciation for the interconnectedness of our world and transformed me into a tree lover. Now, to me, a tree is not just a tree—good for picnics or rope swings or a shady spot to read a book. It is so much more!

Meg still enjoys a good climb, 2017.

Heather and Meg explore the Amazon canopy in Peru.

RAINFOREST MAGIC

A Look at Layers, Leaves, and Life in the Amazon

Imagine you are a visitor in the Amazon rainforest in Peru looking up at a tree. Would you ever guess that it could contain thousands of insect species and many other animals? The rainforest is filled with life! There are four different layers, and each forms a habitat for a different group of plants and animals. Working together, these layers are the engine that supports the rainforest and life on earth.

175 FT.

150 FT.

125 FT.

100 FT.

Scarlet Macaw

Ringed Kingfisher

Howler Monkey

Yellow-Headed Caracara

Kapok Tree

Channel-Billed Toucan

Blue Morpho Butterfly (Female)

Emergent Layer

The very tallest rainforest trees break through the canopy to form this layer. These trees battle hot sun, strong winds, and drenching rain, so the leaves are small, waxy, and tough, for protection and to conserve water. The extreme weather and unstable branches make this a challenging place for animals to live.

Canopy

Tree branches in the canopy reach out to access as much sunlight as possible, creating a wide area for plant growth, fruits, flowers, and animal habitats. Many leaves have a drip tip. This keeps the leaf dry and healthy by allowing the rain to run off quickly. There are lots of epiphytes (plants that grow on other plants), including bromeliads, which can hold water for frogs, salamanders, and insects.

75 FT.

50 FT.

25 FT.

Walking Palm Tree

Cecropia Tree

Cat's-Claw Vine

CAN YOU FIND?

Millions of indigenous people use the rainforest as their superstore.

Remo Caspi: trunk for canoe paddles; bark cures malaria

Kapok Tree: fibers for pillow and mattress stuffing

Walking Palm: trunk for floors, walls, and hunting spears

Aguaje Palm: leaves for roofs; fruit for juice and desserts

Palm Weevil Larva: a tasty treat — grilled or raw!

Cat's-Claw: used to treat arthritis and prevent cancer

Jergón Sacha: underground stem to cure snake bites

Capuchin Monkey

Three-Toed Sloth

Remo Caspi Tree

Jergón Sacha

Poison Dart Frog in a Bromeliad Tank

Shovel-Tailed Lizard

Aguaje Palm Sapling

Tapir

Understory

Leafy bushes, tree trunks, small trees, and climbing vines make up the understory. Saplings (young trees) wait for an opening that will let in sunlight — their chance to make it to the top. The understory is darker and more humid than the canopy, perfect for tropical plants with larger leaves.

Cacao Tree

Boa Constrictor

Iguana

Armadillo

Palm Weevil Larva

Leafcutter Ant

Forest Floor

It might seem quiet, but there is lots of action on the dark, damp forest floor!

Covered with soil, dead leaves, and fallen plants, the forest floor is where life begins and ends. Termites and other small organisms break down material, and then soil fungi take any nutrients and transfer them to plant roots just below the surface.

BIBLIOGRAPHY

Biba, Erin. "Awesome Jobs: Meet Meg Lowman, Tree Canopy Biologist." *Adam Savage's Tested*, September 9, 2014. tested.com/science/464599-awesome-jobs-meet-meg-lowman-tree-canopy-biologist/.

Lasky, Kathryn. *The Most Beautiful Roof in the World: Exploring the Rainforest Canopy.* San Diego, CA: Gulliver Green / Harcourt Brace, 1997.

Lowman, Margaret D. "Before They Were Scientists: Meg Lowman." Interview by Lea Shell. *Your Wild Life*, May 16, 2014. yourwildlife.org/2014/05/before-they-were-scientists-meg-lowman/.

_____. Email correspondence with the author. 2016–2018.

_____. Interview by the author. February 20, 2017.

_____. *It's a Jungle up There: More Tales from the Treetops.* New Haven, CT: Yale University Press, 2006.

_____. *Life in the Treetops: Adventures of a Woman in Field Biology.* New Haven, CT: Yale University Press, 1999.

VIDEO

Lowman, Meg. "How I Climb Trees to Save Forests: Meg Lowman at TEDxNCSSM." YouTube video, 19:14. Posted by TEDxYouth. April 22, 2013. youtube.com/watch?v=zQ2CYq5RlFQ.

———. "Life among the Treetops, Dr. Meg Lowman." Interview by Mariette DiChristina. YouTube video, 26:40. Posted by Google Science Fair. August 15, 2014. youtube.com/watch?v=qTb5SJVgxOU.

———. "Out on a Limb: Challenges of Women in Science." Elon University, Voices of Discovery video, 47:55. March 2, 2016. blogs.elon.edu/ondemand/voices-of-discovery-meg-lowman-ph-d/.

WEBSITES

Margaret D. Lowman, canopymeg.com.

SOURCE NOTES

The source of each quotation in this book is found below. The citation indicates the first words of the quotation and its document source. The sources are listed either in the bibliography or below.

"We are part of our ecosystem . . .": Lowman, *It's a Jungle up There*, p. 265.

"We had already been to the moon . . .": Lowman, "Before They Were Scientists."

"It pained me . . .": Lowman, from untitled unpublished manuscript.

"I was literally the only one . . .": Lowman, "Before They Were Scientists."

"I was frozen with fear.": Lowman, email to author, August 17, 2016.

"From then on, I never looked back . . .": Lowman, *Life in the Treetops*, p. 16.

"[Trees] can't run away . . .": Lowman, "Life among the Treetops," 3:15.

"I found these times alone . . .": Lowman, *Life in the Treetops*, p. 24.

"To my amazement and delight . . .": Lowman, *Life in the Treetops*, p. 29.

"The climb seemed never ending.": Lowman, *Life in the Treetops*, p. 145.

"If we do not conserve rain forests . . .": Lowman, *It's a Jungle up There*, p. 73.

"Plants gave me a voice!": Lowman, email to author, March 11, 2018.

"Now, first and foremost . . .": Lowman, *It's a Jungle up There*, p. 79.

"If only I could have achieved . . .": Lowman, *It's a Jungle up There*, p. 264.

"taking the road less traveled . . .": Lowman, *Life in the Treetops*, p. 205.

ACKNOWLEDGMENTS

I am deeply grateful to Meg Lowman for her inspiration, wisdom, and friendship, as well as for the countless hours she spent answering my questions and reviewing the text. Many thanks to tropical biologist Christopher Frost and Peruvian biologist Pamela Montero Alvarez for ensuring the scientific accuracy; my Amazon guide Ricardo Rengifo Gonzales for teaching me so much about the rainforest and helping me with the back matter; and my editors Carolyn Yoder and Mary Colgan for their brilliant insights and steadfast support.

PICTURE CREDITS